What Daddy Never Told Me

7 Conversations Every Parent Should Have With Their Child

David A. Veney

ISBN:0692278478
ISBN-13:9780692278475

DEDICATION

To my daughters Tyra and Azariah. With each thought of the two of you I realize how unworthy I am to be called your father. It amazes me how God will entrust the most precious things in the hands of the most unlikely caretakers. I make no excuses for my mistakes nor will I seek glory for any "triumphs". The truth is everything good about me is motivated by my desire to make the two of you proud of me. The value the two of you have added to my life is incomparable. I am learning to be better because you already are. I vow to love, protect and cherish you "Till Forever Ends".

CONTENTS

I.

ACKNOWLEDGMENTS

I am so honored and amazed to be able to say that I have completed my first book. This was not something that I planned to do initially. I have been told by so many people that I have a story that needs to be heard but I found it difficult processing through the most effective way to convey it. Mrs. Diana Banks started the process some years ago buy gifting me with a small digital recorder and instructions to just talk it out. Thank You! Although it was some time ago, the seed has finally sprouted. My family, my backbone, who has supported and pushed, irritated and motivated me to completion. You all will forever be the pillar of my life. Aundrea, Michelle, Angie (Beanie), Dionne, Tony, Kris, Angie, Mom and Dad, you all have not waivered and have been patient with me. Thank You! This was all just a thought, a dream, a possibility but I was pushed and it all came together when I actually saw the final production because of the work of Ms. Sheila A. Benson. I so appreciate your attention to detail in the whole editing process. Thank You! So much could be said to so many people but few have walked through the process with me. G. Mandel Copeland, your push, your encouragement, and your brotherhood is a rare thing IT IS TIME! Thank You! Latoya A. Benson, you saved my life! You are a gem and I am grateful for your ability to see beyond the surface and pull out what others chose to ignore! The world is waiting for you let's get it! Thank You! Michael C. and Israel Bell, Mom and Dad Bell; Jaime Crawford and the Crawford family, Durrell Babbs and the Babbs family (hey Baby Luv), Warren Jones

i

and family, Avery Cotton, Maurice Mayo and family, Lonny Wortham, David Creamer and family, Edwin Ballard, I love each of you and I would not have made it through life had you all not been a part of it. I promise to make you all proud and it just gets better from here.

1

...WHO BOB WAS

In my eyes he was a giant. Though he only stood about 5 feet 9 inches with a little more fat than muscle, to me he was an indestructible beast. He was superman on steroids! His presence alone gripped the hearts of people and caused them to come to attention. His charm was the definition of "swag". With a smile that would seemingly

infiltrate the spaces of your despair, he
would speak with words of wisdom so
simple and plain that you wouldn't realize,
until after the conversation was over, that
you just received the worst verbal thrashing
ever and you loved every minute of it. He
was strong and athletic, witty and comedic.
Though he hadn't achieved more than a high
school diploma he could confidently engage
the intellectual and simplify what they had
found complex. He was stern. He had the
ability to give you the whipping of your life
with the stare from his eyes. He was a God-
fearing preacher who would serve the people
with no thought of his own needs. He was
always available at a moment's notice to
answer the call of someone who was in

distress or just needed prayer. He was just that kind of guy. He was my father and though he was all those things, I never knew him.

Growing up I always heard stories about him and how he was this great athlete and the girls went head over heels for him. I saw pictures of him as a young sergeant in the Air Force, pictures that would cause me to question whether or not I had existed in a past life because the resemblance was uncanny. I knew where he was born and how many sisters he had and that somehow he and my mother met and got married. I knew he was a preacher and that he was in the military even though I never knew what he did in the military. I knew he loved music and loved to sing and that at some point prior to him enlisting, him and his sisters sang as a family and were well known. But I never knew him and yet I found myself bound by this unspoken commission to prepare to fill his shoes but how can that happen when I don't even know what size he wears. I would always hear, you look just like your father or you're going to preach just like your daddy. People I didn't know would come and say things to me about how I was just like my father and none of it made since to me because I didn't know him.

Now I know that the lyrics of this song sound exactly like the refrain that has been bellowed from the mouths of millions of children who have been brought up in single-parent homes where mom carried the burden of being mom and dad because the sperm donor abandoned his seed. However, this is not the same ole song. To the contrary, my mother and father married a few years before my birth and have remained married ever since, which is why the situation was so complex.

From the outside looking in, our family was the example of what a happy Christian family should look like. We were the inspiration for the Cosby show. Though we were not "well-to-do", we were all right. And by all right I mean that we didn't starve although there were plenty of nights when sticks and stones (hot dogs and baked beans) were the entrée and dessert for the evening.

If I didn't know any better, I would have sworn up and down that we owned stock in Kenny's shoe store because whenever we were fortunate to get new shoes, when your turn came around, it was always something from Kenny's; probably a pair of Stadia's. Because there were four children (two girls and two boys) in the house at the time, we were pretty much the main attraction for all the other kids in the neighborhoods we lived in. Mom would cook and maintain the house. After we got a little older she did have a job or two and later provided home day care services. We were the good active church members who attended every service, every Bible study, every meeting , every choir rehearsal, every Sunday at Sunday school, and there for Sunday evening Y.P.W.W. (Young People Willing Workers- it's a C.O.G.I.C thing) We did not miss anything. It didn't matter how late the service ran we were there until the very end! So everyone saw us as committed members with this great passion and zeal and dad led the way.

The people, both young and old, loved him and dad loved them. I remember being told how lucky I was to have a father like him and how some of the kids wished that he was their dad. Little did they know, the man that they had come to love so much was a stranger to his family. The man that they could confide in and get advice from was only a voice from a back room in his home.

He was the voice behind the door that would either grant or deny permission to do things that, for whatever reason, when we asked mom she felt the need to respond, "Go ask your father". And most times, the desire we had to do whatever we were asking would magically diminish probably because of the anticipated questions that would precede the answer. Questions like, is your room clean? do you know what time it is? didn't you just? or don't you hear me on the phone? all of which, the majority of the times, seemed to lead to the always dreadful, frightening "No!"

It was a strange thing, seeing him interact with people in the congregation at church. He was the "go to" guy, the life of the party, the backbone, and the answer to everyone's problems, but in his home he was only known as the disciplinarian who did his job well. He would stand in church and preach and the congregation would hang on every word while at home his children, most times, would be terrified to hear him speak. He was always the one that stood out and everyone naturally gravitated to him. But then we would go home and the social butterfly would retreat to his cocoon and seemingly become a completely different person. I noticed, however, it wasn't just limited to church.

There were times when we would ride with dad somewhere on the Air Force Base and the reception he would receive would be

the same as it was when we were at church. I
remember being with dad one day and a
white gentleman started walking in our
direction. I am not sure if, initially, my father
saw him or not but this guy came over and
then started his greeting, "Hey Bob!" It was
the most confusing thing in the world to me
at that time. This white guy just called my
father Bob. I thought to myself who is Bob,
that's not my dad's name, and nobody calls
him that. But dad chatted with the guy for
several minutes. I was blown away. Who is
this Bob guy?

It was as if there was a completely
different person that would take over
whenever dad left the house. I couldn't
understand it. Maybe it was! Maybe in the

house he was just dad and dad didn't do the things Bob did. But this Bob fellow was intriguing and I wanted to know him and even more than that, I wanted him to be my dad and dad could just go away. Don't get me wrong, there were times when dad would allow Bob to come out and spend some time with the family. Those were the times when I could enjoy what other people enjoyed about my dad. Like in those times when we went to amusement parks and things like that or if we had company at the house. We would have a blast! Dad would be the biggest jokester ever. Those would be the times that just seeing him laugh would crack me up. I mean he would make us laugh to the point where it hurt! But as soon as we got home or the company was gone it was business as usual. There would usually be an order given and then off to his room. It was like Bob got dropped off somewhere and wasn't allowed to come into the house or he had to leave when the rest of the company left.

It was an unfortunate thing because Bob seemed like the kind of guy that I could relax around. The kind of guy I could talk to about anything, after all, everyone else could. It wasn't that I wanted "Bob" around because I didn't like the fact that dad was a disciplinarian and I thought "Bob" would let me do whatever I wanted. I wanted "Bob" around because there was something about him that I could identify with. I wanted to be like "Bob" and was like him in many ways.

Among my peers, I was the life of the party, the "go to" guy, the one who the other kids would come to if there was a problem. That's who Bob was and I could easily see that part of me in him, but I couldn't see anything of me in dad. Partly because I rarely saw dad and when I did it was as he passed from the door to his room or from his seat in front of the television to his room. So if there was a part of dad in me, I didn't know it because dad never opened up to me.

I understand that there is a degree of separation that needs to be in place when it comes to a parent and child relationship. It should be clearly understood and represented that the role and mentality of a parent and their child is different. However, even with that understanding, in my opinion there should also be a middle ground where parent and child meet and it is at that place where true nurturing takes place. So many parents make the mistake of being extremist and become either the best friend that "kicks it" with the child without any boundaries or limitations or they are the parent that rules with an iron fist. The former, the "BFF" parent, while being the one that the child relates to on the level as an older friend that is cool to hang around, runs the risk of stripping themselves of the respect that is justly due them and, in essence, removing themselves from a position of greatness that the child one day desires to ascertain. In other words, how can I look up to mommy or daddy when it is clear that we are on the same level? The latter, the warden or the iron fist parent, does everything they can to ensure that the boundaries that they have set aren't crossed thereby creating a negative divide between parent and child and stripping the child of the liberty to just be, while robbing both parent and child of the beauty of relationship. The common thinking in this type of parenting is that, "I need to teach you to respect your elders." It is definitely a dictatorship based on the premise that because I am the parent and I have experienced life and I pay the bills the only thing that matters is what I say, and so you must do what I say and you will understand it one day. It reminds me of the saying made famous by Cliff Huxtable, "I brought you in this world and I can take you out". One of the many problems with that line of thinking is that what the warden calls respect is actually fear and there is no love or true honor in being afraid of someone. And the truth of the matter is that I was afraid of dad, but Bob was someone it seemed I could respect.

Just like with anything in life there must be a balance that is maintained, even in parenting. Finding the middle ground is a task that many have failed at but is attainable by all. Being able to be the shoulder that provides comfort while yet being the strong arm that gives discipline, without compromising the integrity of the intent of the parent child relationship, is something that the child must have and the parent must be able to achieve.   Having said that, I am not suggesting that my desire to know "Bob" was a desire to be best buddies with no honor or respect for him as dad, but I am suggesting that had dad allowed me the privilege of having insight to who Bob was, my honor and respect for him as dad would have been that much greater which in turn would have produced a greater respect for who I was or, better yet, for who I was to become.

This access to that insight can come in many forms and will not happen in just one conversation. It is a constant unveiling of the parent before the eyes of the child. The beauty of the parents' unveiling of themselves is that it will ultimately become the child's revealing of their own selves.

2

...WHERE DID I COME FROM?

I suppose the desire of any father is to have a son that will be somewhat of a reincarnation of himself. A son is an extension of the father and it is a gratifying experience to be able to groom and root on his seed as it grows and excels on its journey to accomplish and achieve more than what the father was able to in his lifetime. I have also found that for a father the desire for a

son is something greater. A son is a

namesake; not necessarily a junior but

someone who carries and continues the

legacy of the name. There is nothing greater

to be desired than the legacy of a good name.

A biblical proverb says that having a good

name is better than attaining riches. The

mark left by a name is how one will be

remembered after the physical person has

passed on. To some this is a great honor, to

be the conduit of legacy. To know that from

your seed the world will be blessed to have

another generation of Harris' or Hopkins or

Kennedys or Rockefellers. For me, however,

this had become an unsettling wrestling

match in my mind. My father was the only

male child of nine children and I am the last male to carry his name and so I found myself at an impasse. As much as I desired a son, the haunting question had become, do I want a son to carry on a name that I know nothing about? And an even more relevant question was how I can carry on a name that I really don't know anything about.

As a child, I was proud to be associated with the name Veney because the Veneys were known as a great talented musical family and it seemed that everyone loved them and because I was a Veney that meant that everyone loved me. How beautiful is the naivety of a child. At the time, I hadn't figured out that I was in need of something from dad and being recognized as a part of his family seemed to momentarily fill the void. I would go and visit my grandmother and spend time with aunts and everywhere we went I would stand with the biggest grin on my face as people recognized me because of who my father was or because my last name was Veney. I would always hear the words "oh that's Anthony's son" or "you're one of those Veneys". During those times it meant something to carry the name Veney. It gave me, as a young boy, a since of belonging and worth. One of the reasons I loved visiting that little town in Maryland was because that's where my name meant something, it's where I meant something. I didn't have to worry about it being mispronounced or somebody turning it into an insulting rhyme to make fun of me. It was Veney, Reet's grandson and Anthony's boy. However, when it was time to return home, I was David Vinnie or Beanie or Vinay and just like a one hit wonder my fifteen minutes of fame had expired.

I remember sitting in classes at the beginning of a new school year and the teacher would ask, "Veney, is that Italian?" and to save myself even further embarrassment I would answer in the affirmative not truly knowing whether it was true or not. There was even a period of time when I adopted the last name of an aunt to avoid the ridicule and shame that came with having the last name Veney. Because I could not explain the origin of my last name and had no idea what it meant, if it meant anything at all, I was willing to abandon my "identity" without knowing who I was. The adopting of another name was just another way to try to escape and find me. At this point what I didn't know about my name and what wasn't revealed to me about who my father was started to cause resentment to build up. I was trapped and the only way out was through the discovery of who I was and I couldn't know that without knowing my father. And so not only did I want to disassociate myself from the name that had been handed down by my father, I wanted to separate myself from any characteristics that caused people to say "you are just like your father". And so I began to do things quite different than what everyone had become used to seeing from me.

I became aggressively violent toward peers finding any reason I could to start a fight. I went from being a straight A student to not putting any effort at all into school work which resulted in my grades dropping drastically. I made a valiant effort to rebel against anything that was told to me by dad. I had a chip on my shoulder and made sure that everyone knew it. I remember dad telling me that people wanted to embrace me and do things for me but were afraid to try because they didn't know how to deal with my attitude. He said that they felt like they were walking on egg shells when they came around me. When I heard that I think it was one of the most gratifying moments of my childhood. People were feeling about me the way I was feeling about my dad and even with all of the defiance, I still could not escape the mark of the name. My behaviors and attitude had changed but I still looked like my father and my last name was still Veney. There was no escaping it.

The feeling of being trapped grew and the desire for separation, birthed from the neglect of the need for inclusion, caused me to live out this fantasy of being a magician who could, at any given moment, disappear just to escape the reality of not knowing. This was a reality that I recognized early on. I would say to myself I just don't feel like I belong here. I felt as if I had been misplaced.

Like the family that I had was not the family I belonged to. Most would say well every child feels that way because he or she just wants their way and they think they can get it somewhere else. For me it was something more. I felt like I didn't belong because I felt as if I were a stranger in the place I called "home" and so I did something about it. I would leave. And this was something that started at a very young age.

I remember the very first time I ran away. I had to be about seven or eight years old. I had spent the night before packing a large suitcase and even wrote a goodbye letter. I had planned it all out. Saturday mornings we wouldn't see mom or dad until about 10 o'clock or so which gave me plenty of time to hop on my bike and go! And that's exactly what I did. I left my letter, told my sisters goodbye, mounted my huffy with my 75lb. suitcase and I was off. However, there was a huge flaw in my plan. In saying my goodbyes, I revealed to my sisters that my first stop was going to be at a friend's house nearby. Imagine the shock when, after being so meticulous in my planning even to the point of hiding my bike in my friend's shed after arriving to his house, we hear a knock at Scott's door and see my father's car in the driveway! Needless to say, Scott was terrified and wanted no part in any of this as he quickly turned me in. I walked out in utter disbelief. How did he find me so quickly? That question was answered as soon as I saw my dear sisters in the car with the most deceitfully caring look on their faces. In the end, I got the whipping of my life and realized I couldn't escape the name and I couldn't escape the man.

As comical as that story has become to me, it was the first real sign of a chase that would continue for many many years to come; a chase that kept me coloring the same circle only in different shades of gray. A chase that, even if it had ended, I wouldn't have known how to recognize the prize at the end because what I was chasing after was identity. Unfortunately, identity was just as much a stranger to me as a homeless man on a corner asking for spare change. I was trying to figure out who I was, where I belonged and how am I different from every other person who walks the face of this earth. What is it about me and what I have in me that will cause people to remember my name and cause my children to be proud to bear the name of their father? At the ripe old age of eight I didn't understand that I couldn't really know that without knowing where I came from and the answer was locked away in this vault who was known to me as dad.

There is a saying that resounds in today's society. A society which is filled with single mothers who oftentimes struggle with trying to raise a male child, that says it takes a man to raise a man. I will take it a step further and say that it takes a father to produce a legacy. This is not to disregard or belittle the ability of a mother however, in all that she does and in all that she is able to accomplish with regard to her son, she will always be nurturing and cultivating the seed of the father. Regardless of the situation or circumstances surrounding conception the truth is that this is the seed of the father. Whether the father is a physically active part of the child's life or not he is still a part of the makeup of the child. It will show in physical, behavioral, and emotional traits. It is that part that the mother can identify with but not completely relate to. It is the part that will frustrate her to the point of saying "you are just like your father" even though he is not present. This absence of the father is a misfortune that will retard and stunt the growth of the child because there is, in my

opinion, a sense of awareness that can only

be passed on by a father. It is not so much an

awareness about what is going on around

you, but an inner awareness about who you

are that brings clarity to what is going on

around you. Daddy never brought that

awareness to me and so because I did not see

myself clearly; my perception of the things

around me was distorted. I never

understood my value and so nothing or no

one around me carried any value to me. I

treated people and things as if the only

purpose they served was mine in that

moment. If I did not see the immediate

benefit then you or it was useless.

With this mentality, I had become the

victim of identity theft by my own hands. Without daddy sharing himself with me in order for me to know who I was, I was forced to create my own me. As you can imagine the results were detrimental. I recognized qualities that I had but didn't understand how to properly use them and so they were used to further my own distorted agenda. It was like the movie "Hancock". I realized that I possessed some pretty cool abilities but something was missing and because something was missing, those abilities caused more harm than good. And it all stemmed from me not knowing who I was because I had no idea of where I came from.

It was a very interesting parallel. Growing up with my father in the military we, of course, were stationed in different places for periods of time. This meant that every few years we were on the move and the same question would come with every move, "where are you from?" Of course I knew I was born in Maryland but if people started asking questions I couldn't give accurate answers because as a young child I hadn't spent much time there and so the only thing I knew at the time was the name of the city and state where I was from. In the same sense, if asked, I could only give vague information about my father because I hadn't spent much time with him finding out. I could simply tell you his name with very little to add to it. One might say as a child that's all you need to know and to that person I ask, then how important is it to know your parents and your heritage with regard to the development of the child and the cultivation of what the child possesses inside of them which was imputed by the parents from the time of conception? I am not suggesting that finding one's self without knowing one's parents or heritage is an impossibility, but I am suggesting that the struggle and loss of time would be minimized if the parent would take time to reveal these things to the child. How different life would have been if I had someone to help navigate through the trails of history as I journeyed to discover who I am.

David A. Veney

3

...ISOLATION IS NOT INDEPENDENCE

It's amazing to me how much of an impact my dad had on me. I never realized that everything I saw him do was a lesson to me. Although they might not have been verbally spoken, they were still lessons. The only issue is that they were lessons that I was left to extrapolate meaning from on my own. As a child, of course, that was extremely dangerous. As an adult, whose perceptions were derived from those lessons, it was detrimental. I became accustomed to that style of teaching and it was evident as I matriculated through high school. Of course, with different courses came different teachers with varying methods of teaching. At the time, I would always prefer the teacher who taught in silence. The instructions were always written on the board and if there was a question, the teacher's response was "it's explained in the textbook." It was the perfect situation to me. The teacher didn't want to be bothered with us and we definitely did not want to be bothered with him or her. I considered myself to be shinier than the average apple and so comprehension was not a big deal, or so I thought. There would be times when I confidently completed a quiz and when the quiz was returned, the grade was counter my confidence. It was all because I somehow misinterpreted the textbook information. The thing that I thought was simple was only simple because there was no one to refute my interpretation. The only way to appropriately apply a lesson is to appropriately interpret the lesson and since my interpretation was wrong, I failed the quiz. This is a problem faced, not just by children, but by people of all ages. For many, the only standard of application is based solely on a private interpretation which could be faulty, thus always yielding faulty results.

Such was the case in my interpretation of independence. Being a male child already surrendered me weak to the suggestion that I can't. In other words, the phrase "I can't" or

"you can't" automatically triggered
something in me that had to prove that "I
can". It was my Achilles heel. If you wanted
to motivate me to do something just tell me I
can't. It was my weakness. This attitude is
referred to by most as pride and others just
call it being macho. I believe that it is innate
in every male to have a certain level of
machismo. In fact, it is essentially necessary.
Think about it. Is there a man that you know
of, who is truly a protector and provider, that
does not exhibit a macho confidence that
actually makes you feel safe? Even if he is
figuring it out as he goes, the confidence or
machismo, that he is displaying makes you
feel secure in the fact that he can handle it.
This confidence is admirably attractive to the

woman and is absolutely amazing to the child. However, such confidence or machismo to the one who is weak and inferior is abhorrently agitating. To me, this was Dad.

I stated early on in this book that Dad was Superman to me. He was Superman and apparently his room was his telephone booth and that's where he stayed. And when he did come out of the room the house stood at attention. It was clear. Dad had priority in the house to whatever was in the house. If he wanted to come out and watch television it did not matter what we were watching the channel would be changed to whatever he wanted to see. If Dad said the stereo was too loud then it must be turned down. It was clear he ruled because he was the authority in the house and he exercised his power in all affairs of the house, from discipline to maintenance. He worked hard and, according to my interpretation, was entitled to the catering that a King receives.

What I did not know then was that seeing Dad this way was developing a misguided understanding of something, my understanding of what it meant to be a man who was independently responsible. Dad displayed everything that a man should be as it relates to being the King or Priest of the home. He was the bread winner. He was the lawmaker. He was the enforcer. He was the example of the man of the house and his presence was always felt even though he was not always physically seen. These were traits that I knew I needed in order to become a real man. In order to rule I must be able to do the things that Dad did. I had to be able to provide and protect; establish and enforce; fix and fortify. But there was another trait. A trait that I don't think I was supposed to pick up but I did. And I think I mastered it without ever paying attention to its existence; it was the ability to intimidate and isolate. I had not intentionally set out to be that way but a mirror has no choice but to reflect the image that stands before it. I was that mirror and Dad was the image I reflected. Parents often want to take credit for the success of their children but will quickly find another source to blame when it comes to the things that aren't necessarily attractive. Parents must realize and understand that at the core of every behavior their child exhibits is a resemblance of the parent. No, it may not be something that you did specifically and it may seem like something worse than anything you would ever do but at the root lays your DNA. People were uneasy around me because, without knowing it, I was reflecting what I saw in Dad. No, Dad was not a bully or anything but the way I internally interpreted his behavior in the home caused me to incorrectly apply things in the way I conducted myself publicly. I understood that a man is independent however; I did not correctly interpret what independence was. I knew that Dad was

independent but what I reflected was a
perception of independence that suggested
that not needing anyone, but instead
everyone else needing me, was what defined
independence. I had, unknowingly, begun to
internalize that being independent was
proven by how well one could function on
his own island. And so it was that vantage
point that gave direction in my quest for
independence. I began to isolate people as if
it was a part of my chemical makeup and it
was supposed to be this way naturally. Just
like Dad, when I came in a room people
stood at attention. I was unknowingly
mimicking or reflecting what I saw every
day. It was not a strategically developed plot
to carry out; I simply followed the influence

that was around me. My grandmother used to say, "If you hang around dogs you will always come away with fleas." This simply means that the thing that you "cling" to or the thing that influences you will rub off on you whether you intend for it to or not.

Dad was the example I looked to. I was learning how to behave through observation and not just through discipline. To this very day there are things that I do, that are exactly what Dad does. I have certain mannerisms and movements that are natural for me; but they are a direct result of Dad's influence. If I carry some of those things now, as a grown man, imagine what was taking place as an undeveloped youth. It was not intentional to brush people off, most times. It was simply a reflection and a distorted interpretation of independence. What I didn't understand, and what Dad didn't convey to me, was that a key attribute of one who is independent is the ability to forge relationships that will later become resources when a need presents itself. I only understood independence to mean that I can do it all by myself. It never occurred to me that relationships are imperative to existence. Now before you yourself misinterpret something, let me be clear. The ability to forge relationships that will later become resources does not imply that you are trying to gather people to form bonds with just to meet your own selfish goals or desires. A friend is a resource. Relationships are, or should be, resources. If you have a true friend whom you can call on in times of despair then that friend is a resource of comfort or encouragement. In the same way, if you have established a relationship with a successful business person, when you are ready to pursue entrepreneurship they will be able to guide you through the proper steps so that you also will be successful. It is not using anyone if you are in relationship with them and you pull on them for strength, support, or whatever else the need calls for. Just be sure that the pulling is reciprocal. If you have a friend and it seems like you are always the one doing the pulling, find a reason for them to pull on you.

And so, as a youngster the understanding

of the need for relationship building was not there because of a misinterpretation and, of course, this misinterpretation only led to other issues in the home. I went from an incorrect interpretation to a completely wrong application and I began to act from the distorted viewpoint that this independence afforded me certain privileges in my parents' home. I began to act as if I were the King of another King's province. It began to be the twentieth century version of the story of the prodigal son found in the New Testament of The Holy Bible. My thought of entitled independence was in conflict with the head of household and recognition of that caused me to do what any defeated King would do, retreat. I would leave the house not only to assert my independence but also to find it. The problem with that was I was in search of a place where I would not be bothered by other people, and I had the ability to do what I wanted to do as an independent individual. I soon found out that the only place where that existed for a fifteen year old black male was in the confines of his own mind while he wondered aimlessly through the streets being invisibly seen by those who he would pass by. I would end up in environments where intimidation and isolation were essential for survival and since I had involuntarily mastered those skills I fit in well.

The problem became that there was this void inside that I could not figure out nor could I fill it. I wanted to be able to freely enjoy being me, but yet be attached to something. That made absolutely no sense to me. It was probably the biggest conflict I had within myself. I had this idea of what independence was, but I craved to be connected. The reflection of the image in the mirror had become a mask and, fear of the real me being seen had caused me now to isolate people even the more. The funniest part of it was that it seemed like this wall of intimidation and isolation got me attention. The thing that I thought would keep people away was now drawing people to me. I would sit quiet, not saying anything to anyone, and it always seemed to catch people's attention. Maybe my interpretation was right on and people could recognize my independence and this is what was drawing them. Of course everyone did not appreciate the application of this self-interpretation. The ones my age-thought I was just a loner but to the older crowd it was something else. Only I would give the impression as if I was allowing them in. Independence had now become an ability to control how close different ones were permitted to get to me, or so I thought. Even with this false sense of control there was still this longing to be connected and that longing seemingly had more power than the desire to be isolated. The reason for that is simple. We were created to be relational beings. Isolation is not normal to our construct and it does not prove independence.

I had to learn the hard way that isolation only resulted in a complete detachment from any person that may have possessed anything that I needed to effectively survive. In the end, isolation left me alone and hurting because what isolation does is burn bridges over things that you will have to cross at some point in life. Of course I did not see that as a child and it was not shown or told to me to be any different. Developing true friendships, even later in life, became a difficulty because my mind had misinterpreted independence and that is what I strived to be.

As parents, the goal in child rearing is so that the child will become a respectably successful adult who positively impacts their world after they have left the "nest". In our quest to accomplish that goal, we must be careful of our presentation of independence. Independence is much more than just being self-reliant. A child will misappropriate self-reliance and in an attempt to be "independent", isolate everyone including you just because you have only presented being able to do everything on your own as independence. It is important to remember that the phrase, "Do as I say and not as I do", will never work with a child who is defying you in your presence and emulating you in your absence. I don't believe that every action of a parent needs to be explained to a child but it should be clear to the child that at the end of a long work day there is a need for alone time. This alone time is not a time of isolation but of solitude. One who is independent knows when it is time to be alone with their thoughts and meditations in order to reflect and refuel so that they might be more effective. The child's understanding of this will yield a greater appreciation of what the independent person truly is and an understanding of the need of the parent to have "me time". I encourage every parent, take intentional time to refuel but also be intentional and take time to reinforce that independence does not isolate.

4

...WOMEN, LOVE AND CARS

It has been said the two loves in a man's life are his cars and his women. If that is the case I have only found love once. I will be the first to admit that I am NOT a mechanic! My knowledge of cars is, for the most part, limited to the shell of the vehicle. I will clean the car; change a tire, put in some fluids when necessary and that is just about it. I am not putting on brake pads, changing rotors, lifting engines, replacing belts and carburetors, fixing transmissions or clutches or anything else that requires a much deeper knowing than just keeping the car running. That is why I have the personal telephone numbers of a few different mechanics that I try to maintain a good relationship with because if anything serious were to happen to my car; I am going to need to contact the mechanic quickly! My father, however, was much different. Dad could be in the car and hear a funny sound and automatically know exactly what the issue was with the car. Not

only could he identify the problem, he knew
how, or what was necessary, to fix it. There
seemed to be this bond that he had with his
cars that goes beyond explanation. I can still
hear him talking to the car and it would
always seem that the car would respond. His
tone with the car was always one that was
easy and calming as if the car had feelings
that dad was sensitive to. He would either
pat on the steering wheel or the dashboard as
if he were consoling or comforting the car
when it began to do things contrary. It never
failed, when he did either one of those
gestures, the car would cease doing whatever
it was doing that caught dad's attention and
it would be fine until dad had the
opportunity to give it the proper attention it

needed. It wasn't until I got older that I can remember dad starting to allow other people to work on his cars. Even then, he was very particular about who he allowed under the hood. I remember one place in particular which was not a private-owned garage; in fact, I believe it was actually a tire shop. If there was an issue with the car, dad would take it to Firestone and wait for hours for one man in particular. It didn't matter that there were other qualified mechanics that were available to work on the car, dad would sit and wait for his guy. I can remember dad staring as the mechanic would look and see what was going on. It almost seemed like if he heard one wrong clank, he was going to jump in and take the tools from the mechanic and just do the job himself. He cared for and knew his cars intricately.

Unfortunately, that knowledge was never passed down to me. Maybe it was his love for his cars that kept him from sharing. He may have assumed that my young, novice hands may mess something up and so maybe the safety of the now was more important than the security of the future. It is important to remember, parents, that as you are raising your children the wisdom and knowledge that is passed on from you to them is securing your safety for your future. Oftentimes, we can find ourselves in a place of frustration from repeating a lesson over and over again. We may even fear, that in the process of teaching, the student may cause more damage and this frustration and fear will have us do it ourselves to ensure that the thing is done right. As a result, the lack of impartation of knowledge could possibly be the demise of a legacy. Or even worse, it could be the birthing of something else negative that will be illuminated in other areas of their lives.

This became the case with me. Of course, I did not realize it until later but the way I dealt with cars was the way I dealt with a lot of other things in my life, especially women. My knowledge of cars, as I said, was limited to the outer shell. I could tell you what was underneath the hood but I did not know how to treat what was under the hood. I only identified with cars by color, model, make, and year. I knew how to drive manual and automatic but could not tell you if the engine was a four, six, or eight cylinder. I knew when it was time to get the brakes done, thanks to the lights on the dash and the squeaking, but I could not change the brakes myself. I couldn't identify where a specific sound was coming from or why the car took longer to turnover at times than others. It was bad! But as long as the car was driving, I was riding.

That same lack of knowledge, however, infiltrated every other area of my life. I had unknowingly become accustomed to only dealing with things according to its shell. I used the example of women earlier, not just because the title of this chapter is about cars and women but because the same way I didn't have the luxury of getting to know about the intricacies of cars was the same way I didn't have the luxury of knowing the beauteous intricacies of women. I grew up in a house with two of my four sisters and so I was accustomed to having females around. I was born in the best position a young guy could ask for. I was born right smack in the middle of two girls. My older sister was a year my senior and my youngest sister a year younger. This was the perfect placement because I wasn't too young for my older sister's friends and I wasn't too old for my youngest sister's friends. Of course, all that didn't matter too much unless their friends never came to the house because I had an older brother who was every girl's delight. He was older, stronger and light-skinned. I didn't stand a chance. But in time, dark skinned guys were in , he left the nest, and I was the last man standing! But let me back to the topic at hand; I had two sisters who lived in the house and the things that were embedded were geared to how I should treat them. In doing so, I learned how to treat women. But the teaching only scratched the surface. I loved my sisters beyond what can be explained but they were my sisters. What I felt for other females wasn't the same as the love I had for my sisters. I was never told what that distinct separation was or how to deal with it and so I just did what I knew to do, deal with the shell.

My father grew up the only boy of nine children with a mother, who we will just say, was worth her weight in gold. There is no doubt that she had standards and values that she instilled in all of her children, but especially in her son as it relates to the handling of his sisters. Those things were evident in the way that dad dealt with my mother. Things like opening doors, and pumping gas, or always walking on the outside; and never ever putting your hands on them were things that were always shown. It was a given that my sisters didn't have to carry groceries in the house, that was my job. It was clear that ladies were first, even though that rule doesn't apply to sisters. But I knew how to be a gentleman. The problem was that being a gentleman only dealt with the surface things. As I grew older, I would hear it said that I was just a male being a male. In other words, all of those things were just to get what I wanted. But I say it goes deeper than that. It was truly all I knew. You see, when it came to cars I gave the car what was needed to satisfy my own needs although it appeared as if I was taking care of the car. The purpose of making sure that the tank had gas and the tires had air and the exterior was clean and the oil stayed replenished, was only because I wanted to ride. It had nothing to do with a bond that I had with the car like dad seemed to have with his. I wanted to ride and those things were not only necessary for me to get what I wanted, but those things were all I knew about maintaining cars. It was the same way I approached females. I had no problem opening doors or carrying bags and "wining and dining", as they say.

The purpose was not solely to satisfy a desire I had and I did not do those things knowing that they would get a goal accomplished. It was all I knew. Just as it was with the cars, the issue was never the "minor" things. However, if that car started yielding signs and making strange noises that indicated there was something going on under the hood, I would quickly find someone else to take care of that. And after they fixed the problem I would take the keys back and it's back to business as usual. It was the same way with females. I had no problem with going out and enjoying ourselves in whatever way we decided. Good conversations and compliments were natural. But if she started yielding signs and making funny noises about what was going on under the hood, it was time for her to find somebody else to deal with that because I was not equipped. If she started talking about how her heart was feeling a certain kind of way and things were getting deeper than surface, it was off to the shop to let somebody else deal with that problem. I knew how to keep the outside clean (a nice outfit or some shoes), replenish the oil (dinner and an outing), and keep the tank on full (put the nozzle in and fill her up) and I did those things well. Outside of that, I could not deal with what was under the hood. I remember one incident as a teenager. There was a young lady who was in college and we met and started spending time with each other, and we enjoyed being young and spry. Well, one night, after we had entertained each other to the point of complete exhaustion and there was nothing left to do but sleep, I was awakened by some strange sounds. Since she owned a cat I just assumed that it was the cat. The sound persisted and finally I got up to see what it was. As I rolled over, I noticed that the young lady was no longer in the bed. I thought maybe she had heard the same noise and, just as I had decided to do, she was investigating. So I

walked toward the door of the bedroom
where the sound was coming from and to my
surprise there she was curled up in the corner
shaking and crying. I immediately stopped
in my tracks. I asked what was wrong and
the response was one that was a clear
indicator of something going on under the
hood. Later on, we had a conversation about
what had happened. I asked how it got to
that point when we were clear that things
were only supposed to go so far. She
explained something that baffled me. She
said that all of the things that I was doing (i.e.
opening doors, carrying bags, etc.) were
things that made her feel special and before
she knew it her heart was in it. This baffled
me for two reasons. One, these were things

that were innate for me. It took no effort on my part to do them. I had seen and been taught to do them from early childhood and so how something so natural could be so impactful was confusing. The other thing was that I never paid attention to the fact that those minor things had an effect on what was going on under the hood. In the same way that keeping the oil changed and keeping gas in the tank effects the engine, those "small" things that were being shown to the young lady were affecting her heart.

I use this comparison of cars and women because there are valuable lessons of similarities that can be taken from it. It is also a good place to start dialog with a young man who is coming into his own. Just as with cars, there is a certain level of accountability and responsibility that he must be made aware of when it comes to dealing with women and relationships. Just telling your child that if you find out they are having sex you are going to cut off their genitalia is not good enough. Trying to scare them with the reality of sexually transmitted diseases is necessary, but it is not complete. We often limit the responsibility of sex to contraception but, just like maintaining the vehicle that only deals with the shell. Being responsible in dealing with women, whether sex is involved or not, must be explained and it is much more involved than how you treat her. I was only instructed from a disciplinary perspective and the only thing it produced was a desire to outsmart my parents to get or do what I wanted.

It is true that age may dictate the necessity to know but you must continue and maintain through the process of growth so that the level of understanding matches the numerical age or the place of maturity of the one being taught. Unfortunately, my level of instruction stopped at a place that did not keep up with what I needed as I matured. And so I did not know how to appropriately place or deal with feelings as they developed toward females. It had nothing to do with the fact that I was not mature enough to deal with the instructions, it may have been that my father was satisfied with the scare tactic. As parents, we may sometimes feel if we "scare the hell out the child" then we won't have to worry about devilish behaviors. Well let me be the first to tell you "IT DOES NOT WORK". The scare tactic is just another way of dealing with the shell and never inspecting what is going on under the hood. I remember at the age of 15 being in the car with my mother and father to go and speak with a young lady and her godmother because the young lady had gotten pregnant and was claiming that it was mine. I denied it up until the point that we pulled up in front of her house. You see, prior to this particular evening, I was told that I could not see this particular female and she was forbidden from visiting me at my parent's house. I was a sophomore in high school and she had already graduated and so it was a badge of honor to have an older female sneaking in my bedroom window. Yes we had gotten caught several times and the scare tactic didn't quite have the effect that it was supposed to. And yet, even to the point of me admitting that yes, she could be pregnant by me because she was still coming to the house, and I was still skipping school to go to her house, it seemed like my father was committed to the scare tactic. There was never a conversation about the responsibilities of being a parent or even if I thought that I had any type of lasting feelings for her. It was only a disciplinary reaction.

How ill prepared I was when, after modeling what I thought a father should be for two years, the baby was taken from me after being told that it was not my child. Okay, let me back up. The baby was born. It was a beautiful chocolate baby boy. By the time of the birth, there still had been no conversation had about the plans for taking care of the child or anything along those lines. I was already distant in my parents' home and this situation seemingly alienated me even further. I felt as if I was left alone and expected to deal with a situation that I was not prepared for. I am not suggesting that it was my father's responsibility to deal with my responsibility but, I am suggesting that I would have been better prepared if there was some discussion. But since there was no discussion, I latched on to the child and his mother as if they were my only reason for existence. The child became my priority and the mother reaped the benefits. My grades dropped tremendously and so I could no longer play football, which I absolutely loved. I did not have a job and so other means to get money were explored. The child was with me more than he was with his mother. I remember one night I was told by my father that I had to check with my mother to be sure that it was alright to bring the baby home to their house to stay overnight which was, at this point, the norm. It was the most baffling thing ever to me. I never asked him or my mother for help and so I could not, for the life of me understand why I needed to ask permission to allow my child to stay with me as if my parents would be responsible for his care. But again, because there was no conversation about it, it was just a greater riff formed between us. What I didn't realize at the time, and I am not sure if this was the reason for the incident, but my availability to the baby relieved his mother of responsibility. I didn't see that I was experiencing the first real encounter with the "female game". I had no idea it existed. That is until a short while later I received a call from this young lady and she simply stated, "I am getting married and I am coming to get the baby."

The fact that she said she was getting married was not the issue for me. It was the fact that she said that she was coming to get my little man. And so when I called her, my question to her was, "do you really think I would let that happen?" I should have never asked her that! Her response rocked my young world. "He's not yours anyway and me and his real father are coming to get him." Immediately I was infuriated! My only reaction was to hang up the phone. Could this be happening? I was not in a position to fight it and I would rather surrender, for the moment, than to have my "lil' man", at the age of two, experience what would only be a ridiculous display of ignorance as the only parents he knew, at the time, went back and forth over him. And so, about a week later I handed over everything I had that belonged to the child believing that things would turn. I had no idea that a woman could be so hurtful. My knowledge, at the tender young age of 18, was only limited to the shell. It crossed my mind that there was someone else but I figured since I took good enough care of the shell it was enough. But while I was treating the shell, someone else was dealing with what was under the hood. What was even more disappointing was that daddy still never had a talk with me about the difference.

It was some months after the initial goodbye when it became even clearer to me. I received a phone call from the young lady asking if I would meet her and give her some documents that I still had in my possession. I agreed and to my surprise she was not alone.

Accompanying her was the gentleman whom she had since married along with "lil' man". I was absolutely fine with the gentleman. He decided he wanted to be present as she and I spoke and I had no problem with that. But before we were about to say our goodbyes, she asked if I wanted to see "lil' man". I excitedly replied, "of course!" Everything was lovely until "lil' man" got out of the car and when I spoke to him he ran and hid behind the gentleman and called him daddy. I, to this very day, do not know how I made it back to the car without breaking down right then. The child that was hardly ever seen without me was now frightened by the sight of me, not because looking at me frightened him but because he had no idea of

who he was looking at. It was as if it was
Halloween and I donned a mask of a creature
that just appeared out of nowhere. It was as
a result of that moment that I realized that
what was under the hood of the woman was
not nearly as important as what was under
my own hood. Had daddy taken the time to
explain to me that my battery had to be
properly functional before I could jumpstart
another one then maybe I would have been
able to recognize what was faulty under the
hood of the woman because I had given
attention to what was under my own.

And so the most valuable lesson I have
learned is one that is being preached and
shouted by mostly women everywhere.
Before there can be a love that is properly

expressed externally, one must be able to love themselves internally. Without the true internal love of one's self, everything else is simply a dependant, infatuated addiction that will either cripple or stunt your growth.

I had no idea of the affect that situation would have on my life. It was equivalent to not getting the oil changed and eventually the engine locks up and now there you are stuck with no way to move beyond the point where the car broke down. Although I had a desire to experience "love" I could not get past the hurt that I had experienced. And so instead of finding another car to buy for myself, I was satisfied with rentals. The commitment was temporal and whenever I wanted to I could turn the keys back in. Of course, the story of the car is parabolic, but it is no less significant. A distorted or disproportionate approach to a thing, in this case love, will delay in the maturing of an individual in that specific area if it is never aligned properly for that alignment should be done by the parent.

Just as dad was particular about who he allowed under his hood and was adamant that "his guy" work on his cars, your son is entrusting you with what's under his hood. You must take the responsibility as "his guy" and make sure you give him the care, through instruction, that he needs.

5

...BEING T.A.G(GED) DIDN'T MEAN I WAS IT

It was the biggest day of the school year. The whole year long this day would be in the back of every one of our minds. Recess was a competitive time but it did not compare to the intense competition of this day. I was a fourth grader at J. E. Manch Elementary School in Las Vegas, NV and this day was the day that everyone could not wait to arrive. It was field day! It was the Olympics of elementary school. The day when the entire school would close their books and the students became the teachers in the class of competition. But this was not just any other field day. This would be the last field day for me at this school. Dad had gotten orders to go to Egypt for a year and the rest of us were moving back to Maryland so that Mom would have support from our relatives there. My reputation for being a young standout athlete was known throughout the entire school by students and teachers alike. Sixth graders would find me at recess to race because they refused to believe or accept that I could be a faster runner than they were.

Whether it was a football game, a basketball game, kickball or four square, I was the one to have on your squad. And I won't even mention the lines that would form of kids that were waiting just for a chance to beat me at tetherball. I was the man. Or so I thought.

Athletics came easy for me but so did academics. I never thought much of it because it was just something that was innate. I do remember having thoughts about some of the other kids in my class. I couldn't understand why they seemed to be struggling in areas that were so easy for me. Spelling was a breeze. Math was a cinch. My imagination made writing quite simple. Now science was a little different, I just wasn't interested. My grades and ability to quickly comprehend, of course, got the attention of teachers to the point that I was recommended for testing for the Talented and Gifted Program or T.A.G.

T.A.G was specifically designed for students who consistently excelled in their academics and were "ahead of the class". I can remember when they initially brought the program to the school. There were about three trailers that sat isolated from the actual school building and all of the students were trying to figure out what they were for. It was mysterious. And of course, for a bunch of elementary school students, mystery meant intrigue which, in the end, meant possible trouble. I had no idea that I would be one of the lucky few to find out what was lurking behind the doors of those trailers. I was tested and really didn't understand the purpose of my being tested. It was an awkward time, but my parents seemed to be fine and so everything was alright. When I finally understood that I was being considered to be a part of this program, things got a little bit strange for me. While I was excited about possibly being able to finally see what was in the trailers, I was nervous about actually going in the trailers. It meant that I would be pulled out and isolated from the other students and I didn't know what to expect. Unfortunately, although I was accepted into the program, it was short lived because of the move back to Maryland. However, you could not take away the fact that I was T.A.G(ged). I was one of the chosen few who would get pulled away from the normal class work to go into the trailers and do advanced work well above my grade level. It wasn't just normal activities, we were taught differently. We were treated differently. In the trailers, we were actually given snacks that we could eat while we were learning. The teachers weren't as mean. The class wasn't crowded at all and the lessons were fun and even challenging. It was heaven and I was the man. Or so I thought.

All of this happened during my fourth grade year of elementary. I was now not only at the top of the list for academics but there was that athletic thing too. And so now the time had come for me to solidify my illustrious spot as the best in the school at Field Day, my final stand, at J. E. Manch. The day was going according to plan. I had signed up for every individual event I could and was coming out victorious in each one. All of that was just building anticipation for the main event which was the 4x4 relay where classes were teamed against other classes close to their grade levels. The winning class would receive a trophy, a pizza party and bragging rights until the next year and of course each participant would be given that coveted blue ribbon with the words "First Place".

The time had come! Our class had been matched against the other fourth grade classes. As we began to ready ourselves to take our positions I remember laughing at the other teams as they stretched and practiced hand-offs. In fact, I can remember during recess time leading up to this day, the other teams would be on the field practicing for this event. It was that serious! My team would come and find me and ask if we should be doing the same thing but, I would say,"they need the practice, we don't." I remember my gym teacher, Mr. Fred, asking me if we were ready for the relay. My response was, "I am the fastest in the school, and I am always ready." His response went right over my head but I have never forgotten it. He said, "It's a difference between having the best runner and having the best team."

Well, none of that mattered now. The moment of truth had arrived. I laughed and joked with my fellow teammates and then took my position as the anchor. Standing with me was a guy who, had his birth certificate been needed to register for this event, would not have been allowed to participate because he exceeded the age requirements. He actually looked like he belonged in the eighth. I remember him vividly because he came to the school in the middle of the school year and he was somewhat of a bully. My first encounter with him was him running his mouth about how he could beat me running after I had dusted one of his friends. So we raced. He lost.

"You can't beat me fighting though!" So we fought. He lost. And now here we are standing side by side waiting to anchor for our individual classes. The horn goes off and the race is on. Just as I expected, my team is out in front. The pass is made to the second leg and the lead increases and the pass is made to the third leg and tragedy strikes! He must have taken off too soon because he missed the pass! The baton is now on the ground and he cannot seem to grab a hold of it. The other teams have now caught up and successfully made their passes and now Daquan is scrambling to catch up and regain ground. I remember the guy next to me saying , "ha yawl aint winning nothing now." My reply was, "you needed the head start anyway and you still gonna lose." By now the runners are up to us, of course my teammate is pulling up the rear, and we ready ourselves. I am intensely quiet and the moment arrives. This is it! I remember everything I had learned from my brother who ran track for his high school. I looked back to see where my teammate was and started my trot with my arm stretched back to receive the pass. The only problem was my teammate hadn't learned the same lessons and I didn't take the time to share it with him. He reached and I reached and the baton ended up on the ground. So I scramble to recover and now find myself in a strong last place. The other runners were on the straightaway and I had yet to hit the turn. I felt myself tense up which is something that I never did in running. I gave everything I had and was gaining ground quickly. I could hear the screams of the teachers and students and they were pushing me. They pushed me past one runner and that was it. I had finished a strong third place. The first thing I remember hearing in my head was, we should have practiced. There was no question about our individual abilities, but it meant nothing if we didn't know how to work together. So I left that year as the fastest one in the school that lost the relay. My talented and gifted self was not enough to get that blue ribbon and I was not the man.

This seemingly became the theme of the

composition of my life. Ability to get something done was not the issue but I seemed to be missing the key component that would put me over the edge. That one thing that would separate me from all of the other talented and gifted people that somehow would find a way to share in, what I felt, was my own special place. With every move into a new neighborhood or new school I attended, although it was obvious to others that I was T.A.G (ged), I had a hard time being "it". Understand, my quest for being "it" wasn't a desire for a place on the most popular list but I felt that my ability entitled me to things without putting effort into proving I was deserving of them. I had not been directed to the realization that achieving things in life was not based on talent alone. It was a lesson that constantly was presented to me and each time I took the test I failed. Of course, constant failing would lead to constant frustration which would lead to a hearty disinterest in things that came naturally easy for me.

Let me clearly state what I mean by failing. It wasn't that every time I attempted a thing I did not accomplish it. In fact, I would get the job done easily and effectively. However, there was something missing that would prevent me from going to the "next level". If I played sports, I would make the starting team or even all stars if it applied. I was a standout. But again, to me that was enough. While others were working to improve or enhance their skills, I was satisfied with being named with the ones that "did it well" however, me simply knowing my capabilities meant nothing at all to anyone who did not know me and very little to those who did. The best way that I can describe it is to compare it to a sprinter who is now trying to run a marathon. If the sprinter relies solely on his skills as a quick runner in the events that he is accustomed to running and does no extra training for the long distance marathon, he will gas out quickly and not finish the race.

It seemed like I found myself in that place where I would always gas out. I did not put in the training to do anything and relied strictly on my ability to do the same thing I had always done. It became the norm for me in everything. I knew I was intelligent and ahead of the class however, that only worked in the grade that I had passed. Each year or in each situation I would do a dangerous thing, I would measure my future success with tape from a time past. It seemed that Dad did the same as well. He must have assumed that because I was successful in the "prior", that meant I had what it took to be successful in the next challenge. Maybe that is why he never pushed me like other parents did with their talented and gifted children. He never told me that applying myself meant more than just committing to the moment when it's time to perform.

I walked with a silent confidence that was misleading. In fact, it led me to many more defeats than victories. Of course, with more and more defeats came less and less interests. In terms of academics, as the result of not studying in times past because of my thinking that I would be able to do the same thing I always did and ace the work, the work actually became difficult for me. Even when I attempted to study I still could not grasp it. Dad began to tell me I was just being lazy and the work wasn't hard. Those were the moments I would get disciplined for bad grades, but still I could not do anything about it because I was too far gone. I certainly could have been tutored, but it had become more of a mental challenge than anything. I just did not want to anymore. I was full of potential but never developed the drive to be or do better.

Every child is going to be passionate about something. There are going to be areas that they are naturally gifted in. In the school system being T.A.G. was for a select few who stood out academically. In life, T.A.G. is not limited to a few. Placed in front of something the child enjoys, you will quickly be able to see that every one of them are talented and gifted in their own areas of expertise or passion. But you must, as a parent, instill in them that being talented and gifted is not enough. How many young boys have dreams of becoming a great sports figure when they grow up? For millions of those same boys they have the potential to make it. I would venture to say that for over seventy-five percent of them, it's just a natural gifting and outside of the required practice time for the team there is very little time put into perfecting their craft. It is not limited to athletes. Whatever the passion or area of talent is for the child, part of the rearing is to help nurture those other areas as well. It is of the utmost importance that the child knows that it takes disciplined effort to achieve. It has often been said that hard work pays off. If I had the opportunity to speak with whoever coined this phrase, I would humbly ask them to recant. Hard work can be counter-productive to development. It is possible to be working hard doing things the wrong way. In the end, you will have exerted extra energy and wasted valuable time working hard on doing something incorrectly. The child must know and be taught that consistent, disciplined, and proper applications are what render a great pay off and get them to the desired end. This does not in any way negate mistakes; mistakes will happen. There will be times when it seems that they have reached just short of the goal but it's in those times where the need for the reinforcement of the support system must come in to play.

You as the parent are the child's introduction to support. This is a conversation that is dual in nature. It must be verbally spoken and physically shown. Telling them that talent alone will not be enough must be accompanied with your consistent push for them to pursue the better.

I am reminded of a movie starring Samuel L. Jackson called "Coach Carter". The movie, which is based on a true story, is about a spirited coach who was challenged with giving leadership to a basketball team in Richmond, Virginia. The school is an inner-city school and is filled with youth full of potential and hopes of getting out of the "ghetto" based on their athletic abilities. There is a scene where Coach Carter calls a meeting with the parents and submits a contract that must be signed in order for the boys to play basketball. One of the stipulations in the contract was that the boys maintain a 2.3 grade point average. The parents were outraged. They did not understand why the coach was asking for more than what the school system required, which was at least a 2.0 grade point average. Coach Carter, understanding the academic struggle of the school as a whole, reasoned by explaining that with a higher grade point average the boys would not have to score as high on the S.A.T to get into college. Even after hearing his explanation the parents began to say how it was just basketball and their sons' talents would be sufficient to get them into college. Fortunately for those young men they had Coach Carter, otherwise; they would not have been pushed beyond their perceived abilities. They would have fallen victim to their own limited thinking and in the end would have been left with memories of the glory days and potential that never was fully met.

Parents, I encourage you to be your child's biggest fan, but also be their Coach Carter. Push them beyond what comes natural for them. Affirm that they are T.A.G (ged) but help them to become "it".

6

...THE QUALITY IS IN THE FABRIC AND NOT THE LABEL

I have mentioned that we were not as fortunate as other families growing up. We were not privileged to, what we believed, were the finer things in life. We were secure. Stable living conditions. We had ample food to feed all of our greedy mouths. And we were clothed. Even if the clothes weren't what we wanted, we were clothed. It didn't matter what city we lived in Mom could always sniff out the three places that all of our clothes would come from; The Base Exchange, Kinney's Shoe Store, and Montgomery Ward. It is a little sad to say that even a trip to Morton's was a plus. It didn't matter how much time we would spend searching for the perfect shirt or that shoe that looked like the Nikes, when it came time for the public reveal, everybody who was anybody could tell and made it known that what we had was not the popular name brand. Of course, my sisters didn't get it as bad or as often as I did because the rules of engagement seemed to be a little different for females than males back then.

It didn't matter how smart I was or how good I was athletically, the Achilles heel was

always the clothes. It wasn't that I was
picked on a lot but the fact that I had been
picked on at all made it a sore spot. I had
become more aware of what name brand I
didn't have on than other people paid
attention to. I was one of the kids who
would always make up stories at the
beginning of the school year about still
wearing summer clothes the first day of
school because we just had not been
shopping yet. I would say things like, "These
are just my play shoes and I didn't wear my
new ones because I don't want to break them
out yet." Of course, when school starts in
August and by October you are still making
excuses, it becomes obvious that the stories
were all lies and the clothes you have been

rocking are the only clothes you have. That's
when you start saying that the brand you are
wearing, that is really a Montgomery Ward
special sell item, is a famous brand that
everyone else hasn't seen because they don't
sell them in the regular stores.

I will never forget one of the most
embarrassing moments in my childhood was
in the fifth grade during gym class. This was
during the one year that Dad was away in
Egypt and we were living in that small town
in Maryland. It was time to get a brand new
pair of shoes and I wanted some high tops.
Of course, I went through the same routine as
always. I begged and pleaded to go to the
mall to get a pair of name brand tennis shoes
but, of course, we ended up at Montgomery

Ward or it may have even been K-Mart.
Since I had already bragged about getting a
pair of high tops, I went for the first pair I
saw. I don't even remember what they were
but I do know that I tried my hardest to pass
them off like the hottest shoes ever worn. My
efforts were all in vain on this day at gym
time. We were getting ready to play a game
of full-court basketball and as is typical of
any basketball game, before the teams were
picked we were shooting around.
Everything was fine until I decided to stop
shooting jumpers and go in for a fancy lay-
up. I got the ball and began my journey to
the hole. My dribble was great and it was
business as usual until I planted my leg to
jump. In this moment, it seemed like the

laws of physics were against the normal laws of operations. Instead of going up when I jumped I went down, backwards. My wonderful high tops apparently felt more like glass slippers on a wet floor. Whatever material the soles of those shoes were made of did not agree with the hardwood gym floor. I slipped and the whole world saw it and let out a laugh that almost sounded harmonic. The strangest thing about the whole thing was that the laughter and jokes did not separate me from the shoes I wore. In other words, it would have been one thing to have jokes told simply about the fact that I had on a pair of shoes that caused me to slip in a way that I will never forget but, the jokes included me. I was identified by this poorly made tennis shoe. My athletic ability did not matter. My personality was not considered. I was laughed at and looked at because of the shoe I wore.

I was at an age of discovery. While I had experienced being talked about to some degree in times past, there seemed to be an awakening in me that said you have to "look" better to be better. Looking better did not mean that I had to keep my hair cut or make sure my hygiene was superb. Looking better meant that I had to wear the labels. From that point on, I decided to do whatever it took to wear the labels. It started off with simply wearing other relative's shoes or clothes. Then it went from wearing their things to "forgetting" that their things were in my bag and "not knowing" how their things ended up in my room. I don't know if Dad saw the signs of my search or if he just believed they were not serious enough for him to be concerned. There came a time when other people's clothes weren't enough and I had to try to figure out how to have my own. Of course, a kid that young has only a couple of ways to earn money to buy his own clothes and for me cutting grass was not going to do it. Allow me to insert this while we are here. Parents understand that peer pressure is indeed real. While you want to insure that your child knows that keeping up with the "Joneses" will forever keep them in a rat race that does not profit anything, you also need to be aware of the impact unhealthy social experiences will have on them as they grow. If you see your child chasing things that are popular, understand that it is NOT just because everybody else has it. The reason is a little deeper than that. What they are really chasing is acceptance. They, like you, do not want to have to go into an environment where they spend the majority of their time and constantly be ridiculed for what they seemingly have no control over. For them that environment is school but for you, it may be your job.

My chase led to activities that I should have never been involved in but, at the end of the day I was wearing the labels and I wore them well. What I didn't realize at the time was that I was not just wearing these labels outwardly. Because Dad was strict, and there were things that he could pick out if he saw them, I had to cleverly find ways to keep my good clothes separate from the clothes that my parents bought me. I would go so far as to keep clothes at friends' houses and get them whenever I needed to. Well soon that plan proved to be bad because clothes started to disappear or they would appear on the backs of these friends and coincidentally, their parents purchased the exact same items that I left at their houses. I was going through all of these changes to keep the labels.

A problem internally that was taking place was that I now, along with changing clothes, had to change personalities in whatever environment I was in based on the type of clothes I was wearing. Wearing the name brand clothes in certain places brought with it a disposition of being "it". I "fit". Fitting meant that not only that I dressed like the other kids with the good labels, but I also acted the way they did. It was as if the outfit was a total transformation of who I was. My validity came in what I had on, the labels. Little did I know that I had established a pattern that would become the thing that I depended on for many years to come. In the repeating of this pattern, I was fooled by my own acting. I had become a chameleon. I had the ability to change to fit wherever I was. I needed to hear Dad say that the ability to adjust and adapt is a good quality but you must always be able to come back to your original state and be who you really are at the core. Adaptation does not mean, or should never lead to, imitation.

My pursuit for labels on clothing gave way for labels to be put on who I was and just like the clothes, those labels developed and defined me. This labeling was not just based on what I wore. I was labeled by teachers, other adults, and church members alike. It seemed that because I wasn't sure of who I was, I needed the labels to tell me who I was. The issue was that, even if some of the labels were true, I would only present whatever the label was to the person who gave it to me and I could not completely see it for myself. I gave more weight to how people saw me, or labeled me, than I gave to how I saw myself or what I thought I knew about myself. It was during this time that the direction from the one I came from was needed. I needed to be directed to the place where the real me was. I needed to know that it didn't matter what other people said about me because I was more than how they labeled me. Every label wasn't a negative one. However, even the positive labels were of no value to me since I didn't believe I possessed the quality that those positive labels represented. It was as if I was wearing good quality clothes but they were four sizes too big. I did not feel good enough to live up to the labels but I was a good actor. Since I was a good actor, the presentation convinced everyone around me that I believed I was the label. So I was labeled smart but my grades had fallen to below average. I was labeled funny and jovial but when the crowd was gone, I would go into a dark place of despair. I was labeled many things but when I was left alone to be with me, I had become the opposite of every label. Even the not so good labels were wrong. I was labeled by others as standoffish, but I longed for companionship. I was labeled stoic, but my heart desperately wanted to be received and accepted. It didn't matter what the label was. Underneath it all I did not feel, or believe, what others said about me. It was that uncertainty, without the validation of the quality of my fabric that led me down the longest dead end road ever traveled.

I often wonder how different my journey would have been had I been told that there are many people who were wearing the name brand labels but they were knock-offs. I had, in essence, become a knock-off trying to fit in with people who were wearing knock-offs. It doesn't matter what the name on the label says, if the quality of the fabric is not good, it won't be long before the truth is exposed. Holes will appear, shirts will shrink, soles will begin to separate from the shoe, all because the quality of the item is not in the label but in what the item is made from and how it was manufactured. The truth was I possessed the quality to create my own line, with my own label, but I was blinded by what was popular. I was more concerned with looking the part as opposed to being the part.

Parents do your best to affirm the quality of what your child is made of. Affirm who they are more than what they can do. They may be extraordinary in some areas but never allow them to be defined by how they do a thing. When their ability to do a thing has dwindled, they have to know that they are more than their ability or the label. They are not beautiful based on the standards of "industry" people. They are unique and that is what makes them beautiful. You are the first line of defense. Build them up and teach them to properly take care of their quality fabric by you being the first to properly care for their quality fabric.

7

...HE DIDN'T KNOW ME

Anyone who knows me knows that I am the perfect balance of simple and complex; okay maybe not the perfect balance but pretty close (if this was a text message I would insert "LOL" right here). But in all seriousness, those who have taken the time to get to know me will tell you that there is definitely more to David than meets the eye. I have always been the "quiet storm". The one you would underestimate until it was time to perform and after the performance you would always remember the quiet dude that won. I was very unassuming. I only dealt with a select few and it was that select few that would be privy to certain things about me that most didn't know unless there was a reason for exposure. I was never the life of the party except when it was a private party where the guests were those who were close to me. If you ask three different people to describe me, you would get descriptions of what would sound like three completely different people but all three descriptions would be true. I was the quiet smart kid. I was the fast athletic kid. I was the kid that would beat you up if you messed with his friends or his sisters. I was the kid who stayed to himself and the kid who was the best friend to have. I was the kid who would cuss you out and the kid who always knew his bible memory verses. I was all of those things and if there was one person who knew that better than anyone else it was my father; or at least that is what I wanted to believe. After all, I was just like him.

When a father is active in the life of his child there is a level of trust established in the father from the child that, in my opinion, cannot be adequately explained. This trust causes the child to move with a confidence not only in the presence of his father but in his absence as well because this trust has produced something that transcends matter, but manifests itself so that all things physical are affected by it. It comes from a knowing that I have superman in my corner and his name is Dad. It's knowing that dad knows what is best for me and how to make sure that I get it while protecting me from anything that will harm me. This means that even though he knows I don't like peas he finds a way to get me the nutrition I need to be healthy. He knows how far I will go because of the confidence that I have in me and he knows when he needs to push me to get to the place where my confidence hasn't grown to yet. He knows the flaws and the strong suits that I possess and he gives guidance to develop those things in hopes of seeing me become greater than he is. This trust comes from a certainty that dad knows me better than I know myself. At least that is what a child would like to believe, it's what I would have liked to believe.

This belief was one that I possessed and it was empowering but there were times when it would leave me baffled. There would be times when it seemed like I was a distant nephew as opposed to his beloved son. Times when dad couldn't remember my birthday or how old I was. After a while, it just became the recurring joke that dad's memory was terrible. Take hospital visits for example. Hospital visits with dad were not the same as they were with mom. Mom would go in and every question that the doctor would ask she would look at me while answering the question as if she was recalling the moments or periods of time that coincided with the responses she was giving. It was as if she was reliving moments. Dad, would look at me while he was answering questions too, but his reason for looking was much different. When dad was looking at me it was because he was usually asking me to help him remember dates and occurrences that were related to my medical history. It would be the same routine. For instance, the question would be asked, "and how old is the little guy? " Dad would look at me and say ten? I would chime in and say no dad eleven. Then he would say that's right your sister is ten. No dad, she is nine she won't be ten until December. Then there would be a chuckle and on to the next question. It never ever crossed my mind that it was more than just a memory lapse. There was no way that it could be more than that. This is my dad, surely he knows how old I am. Things like this would seem to happen whenever mom wasn't around. Dad would seem to forget that I don't like this or I needed to do that.

Of course, as I got older, there was no need for dad to remember because I could answer for myself or do things myself and it saved every one the embarrassment of dad not remembering. However, the memory lapses would seem to spill over into other things. Dad would forget that I had practice and needed to be picked up. Or forget that there was an assembly at the school and so the embarrassment went to a completely different level. I remember sitting for hours after football practices waiting on dad to come get me because he forgot. It seemed that dad really had a memory problem. I can recall a day when our church had a "men's" outing and so we all went to play basketball. By this time, I was about twelve or thirteen and my brother was about to graduate high school. And so we played and had a wonderful time playing with the old guys. For me however, it was just another day at the office so to speak. This wasn't anything new after all, just about every day I would walk out of the house with a basketball in my hand and go play at a nearby basketball court so you can imagine the shock when, later on in a conversation dad was having with mom, dad says "I didn't know my sons had it in them. I didn't know they were that athletic and they are good. That was the first time I have seen them like that." What! I could not believe what I was hearing. Obviously dad is having another memory lapse. He has just forgotten that my brother was an exceptional football player and ran track. It slipped his mind that even at my young age I had MVP trophies and held records for football. He just forgot that I always made all-stars even when I played baseball, which I'd played since I was about 8 years old. There is no way in heaven or in earth that he just didn't know. Dad just forgot.

From that moment on it seemed that

there was always this question
overshadowing everything that I did and the
question became, "does my dad really know
who I am?" How could he not? I am his
seed. His memories of me go beyond what I
can remember of myself. He has been there
my entire life. How could he not know me?
It is important to note that it was during this
period of time when my trust in my dad
began to dwindle. I could not comprehend
my father not being the one I look to for
guidance and direction in life but yet he
doesn't know me. How can nurturing take
place when there is not a knowledge of what
it is that is there that needs to be nurtured? If
there is not a proper identification of the seed
that is supposed to be cultivated, there is a

great, if not absolute, danger of killing the seed because of improper care. I certainly didn't understand it then but I think subconsciously I became uncertain of my dad's ability to properly develop me and so I gave in completely to the idea of developing myself. What a process that turned out to be!

I have always been the quiet observer. I, since I can remember, would always watch people and how they do things. I was fascinated with their behaviors and would oftentimes know exactly what to do to cause a specific reaction from an individual. It would amaze me how easy it was to push people's buttons for a positive or negative response. In a short amount of time, I could sit and talk with an individual and

confidently tell them after the conversation
was done that "I know you better than you
think I do." I had a gift it seemed and I used
it, I admit, a lot for my own personal
entertainment, but also as a part of my self-
developing, or so I thought. There was a
period of time when I would take what I
observed in other people and tweak it so that
when I did it, the outcome would be
something different. That didn't last long.
The person who I really was would always
prohibit me from living a plagiarized life.
One thing I have always proclaimed is that
you will never ever encounter another person
like me. And so taking pieces of other people
and somehow conforming those pieces into
an image that I called me could never work

because at the core, the real me was too strong to be hidden. The real me had been taught what was wrong and right. The real me thought for himself and was a reflection of something much more glorious than what could be seen in the present moment. The real me had been intricately designed and uniquely fashioned and no matter how dirty the cloak was I used to try to cover me up, the real me would always be seen. And if the world around couldn't or refused to see the real me I still believed there was one person who always would, Dad.

My self-development led me down a path that was ultimately going to be my self-destruction but, of course, I refused to acknowledge that truth as a teenager. My need to find my own way and where I fit in became more evident as I would frequently leave the house for days at a time. I began to fall into a false sense of security that a lack of accountability brings. I developed my own idea of what it was to be a man and since I did, and it was based on my own philosophy, of course I fit the bill and since I was a man by my own standards no one could tell me anything. However, I was still searching for something and so I ran the streets and was introduced to people and things that presented a sense of belonging. I wanted these things and these people more than I wanted anything else and so they became my focus. I did what I thought was necessary to maintain things and keep relationships with these people. The life I was now living was not a counterfeit but a distorted misinterpreted version of the truth. I had boundaries and limitations because no matter what, I could never get away from me. But to see me at this period of time would cause you to think differently. This was the cloak I wore. I am not sure if dad's frustration with it all caused him to forget that the real me was underneath the mask or if he believed the cloak was, in fact, the real me. That question would be answered soon enough.

By this time in my life I had been out of the house for a while and had gotten involved in some things that had gotten out of hand, and in order to find resolve, I

decided to move to that little town in
Maryland where I had been born but knew
little about. My thinking was that since I had
family there I could take some time and
refocus and try to correct mistakes that I had
made already and, in a short period of time,
return to where I called home and start over.
Life in that little town was very different. It
was a breath of fresh air and I think the fresh
air caused me to ignore signs that ordinarily I
would have picked up on immediately. In
any case, I went through a wide range of
things and found myself, eventually, doing
the same things that caused me to come to
that little town in the first place. It was like
the real me had been suffocated by the cloak
and now the cloak had become all that I

knew but I still believed that even if I lost a sense of who I was, there was someone who could remind me. Or maybe that was just the innocence of a child always believing that superman would always be there to save him.

Strange and random things started happening which were not really back to back, but close enough to cause someone to pay attention. Friends and I would have conversations about things in life and things we were doing that seemed way too complex for people our age to even think about let alone understand with certainty and conviction. Some might say it was just because we were "connecting with the earth" on a different level and I may be inclined to agree to some extent, but the truth was there were things going on around us that we seemed to have a keen insight to but we refused to heed the signs. After ignoring all the signs, things for me came to a screeching halt. I received a message saying that I was being searched out by a detective and that I needed to contact him because I was a person of interest in an investigation. Of course, I had no idea what this was about and I remember telling my friend that it must be another one of those strange things that has been happening and so instead of going to the station, I called and inquired as to why this detective was looking for me. When I called the station, I remember hearing the tone in the officer's voice change after I told him my name and I was trying to clear up what must be a misunderstanding of some sort. The officer simply said, "Yes you need to come in immediately!" Since he wouldn't say what it was I didn't pay it any more attention until about a week later.

I had spent the day with someone with whom I had become amazingly smitten with. It was a young lady who was attending one of the colleges in that area and she seemed to be as interested in me as I was in her. We had met only a short time prior to this day but the bond grew intense in a short amount of time. It was about four o'clock in the afternoon on this particular day when we returned to the apartment and it was as if a friend who lived in the same complex had been waiting for us to return because about three minutes after we walked into the apartment there was a knock at the door. I thought nothing of it since it was a young lady that was in a relationship with a friend of mine at the time. What became strange was that she said she needed to talk to me at her apartment and that her boyfriend, my close friend, was going to meet me there shortly. So I told my "girlfriend" that I would be right back and proceeded to leave out of the apartment to walk across the parking lot to the apartment of my friend's girlfriend. Never did I imagine the conversation we were about to have, in a two minute walk, would be one that would rock my world the way it did.

As we walked across the parking lot she informed me that she had received a call from her younger sister saying that I was on a news flash. Of course my immediate response was she just saw someone she thought looked like me but to my surprise as soon as we walked into her apartment, there it was, a picture of me taken about a year prior, with my name on top of it and in bold letters to the right, "WANTED RAPIST". I immediately was stuck where I stood! My pager began to go off nonstop. My mind could not grasp the fact that a picture of me was just on television and they were saying that I had raped someone. I had absolutely no idea how this could be happening and so I needed to have another one of those richly complex moments that only came from being "connected with the earth" on another level.

Once my mind was clear enough, I remembered that in my apartment sat a young lady that I have only known for a short time and she has probably seen the same newsflash that I just saw. And so I headed back across the parking lot to my apartment. When I opened the door she was still there and the look on her face was one that expressed something that, at the time, I didn't understand but I would never forget. I could tell by her look that she had in fact seen the newsflash but she was still there. The look on her face at that moment said I don't know what's going on but I know you didn't do it and that's why I stayed. I began to explain to her that I, at that point, knew just as much as she did and that I did not rape anyone. She only asked how they got my picture. But she said she knew I didn't do it and she wasn't going anywhere.

So together we walked back across the parking lot to my friend's apartment and I can remember there being people getting into their cars and it seemed as if their eyes were burning holes in my chest. I spoke to them as I always did and went on my way as they went on theirs. I think it took a minute for it to really hit me that this was real, I was really wanted for this crime and the police were really looking for me.

So I picked up the phone and I called dad. I called not just to let him know what was going on because, as I soon found out, he had already been informed by relatives that hadn't spoken to me in months. But I also called because I needed to be reassured once again that everything was going to be alright. He was calm and didn't say a whole lot. I told him that I had spoken with a lawyer who advised that I turn myself in as soon as possible and dad said he would come with me. In that moment he was superman all over again to me. Everything I believed about him knowing me better than anyone on earth and knowing what to do to make everything better and knowing how to protect me, everything that I had buried under the cloak of my distorted thinking had now been resurrected. Superman was on his way.

As we sat waiting and trying to figure out what was going on and trying to remember where I was on the day in question, I remember looking over to my "girlfriend" on several occasions and catching eyes and asking her if she was ok and vice versa. I thought it necessary to reassure her that this was a mistake and I did not do what I was being accused of doing, but I would actually get reassurance from her when she would say, "I know." In my mind, I wondered how she could be so sure since we only met a little while ago, but she said she knew and she stayed.

So when dad got there it was almost midnight. I remember two distinctively different conversations, one with my "girlfriend" and the other with my father. The conversation with my "girlfriend" was not what you would expect from someone with whom you have only been acquainted for a short period of time. She asked again if I was alright and then she asked what I needed her to do. I jokingly said don't disappear on me and she in turn asked if I was sure I wanted to turn myself in. Boosted by the presence of my dad, I confidently said that everything is going to be alright and this will be over quickly. She had the most calming look on her face as I stepped out of her car to get into the car with my father to turn myself in.

It is important to note parents, that no

matter the direction your child chooses to go, they always know how to get home. They will always be connected to home because home is where his heart is. Home is where all other facades are put down and they can be free to be themselves, providing you have structured it that way. Home is, or should, be their safe place. It should be the place where, even if approval of certain behaviors is not given, they never feel rejected because home is where everyone can see and knows the real them. When everything and everyone else around has turned away, the child's hope lies in the knowing that they have a place called home. It's not built on a foundation of brick and mortar but it's the comfort and assurance that it's where they belong and will always be welcomed even if they have messed up. If you take that away from them, there is a great probability that you have evicted them, not from a house, but a place of belonging and purpose. After being evicted they are left with no choice but to find a way to survive and it's done with a constant push of remembering the rejection from home. The child's decisions won't reflect where they came from and he or she won't know how to get to where he or she believed they were destined to go. Knowing your child is knowing yourself. That you have instilled values and morals that will always be their compass.

And so I got into the car with dad and we sat for a minute. He asked if I was alright

and if I was sure I wanted to turn myself in. I
answered in the affirmative but we didn't
move. I wasn't nervous at this point.
Superman was here. I had this confidence,
not just because I knew the truth but because
dad had my back. I can't explain how I felt
when he opened his mouth to speak again. It
was as if I had just peaked at the top of the
highest roller coaster and now here comes
the drop. The confidence and assurance that
I was given by dad because of his presence
alone was snatched when he spoke and said,
"I have to ask, did you do it?" I was utterly
shocked! How is it that someone whom I
have only known for a short time in life,
never felt the need to ask if I did what they
were saying I did, but you my father, who is

supposed to know everything about me say you have to ask.

I refused to allow him to see the hurt that his question caused me. And immediately a wall was built between him and me. As we pulled up to the police station that question was the only thing I could hear. How could you ask me that? That kept echoing in my head all the way to the point of being handcuffed and placed in the police car to be processed. Dad really wasn't superman. In fact, in that moment it felt as if he was my nemesis. It was in that very moment, while everything around me was in a downward spin out of control, I realized that the mayday call that I had made was in vain. The super heroic rescuer had arrived but he could not reach me. It was then that I made the painstaking discovery that not only did I not know my dad but my dad really didn't know me.

POST-SCRIPT

By now I hope that you have gotten that the intent of this book was not to cast blame on my father for anything that transpired in my life. To be absolutely clear, my father is still my inspiration. I love him dearly and will sacrifice my life to save his. I have come to the place of understanding that teaches not to hold people to a standard that they have not been exposed to. It is my earnest prayer that through the stories shared of my experiences growing up that you have come to a realization of the importance of being open and transparent with your child as you nurture and groom them to be great assets in society. I certainly would not suggest that this book holds the key to having a perfect relationship with your child however, I do believe that it does lay out a solid foundation from which healthy communication and a sense of self awareness can grow. I am sure you may be saying that it is all easier said than done. That is why I have added this post-script. Throughout this book I have laid out subject matters that I believe will help in making both the child and your relationship with your child one that is healthy and well-rounded.

So how do we start these conversations? I have three suggestions that are very simple.

Of course, there are many ways to engage in healthy dialogue with your child but the following three suggestions are good places to consider starting:

- Create moments that are enjoyable and allow the child to let down their guards.
  - Whether it be a fun family night or just a silly playful moment, make it a teachable moment. I do warn against having a serious conversation attached to every fun moment. Those moments will quickly become dreadful as the child will quickly associate those moments with lectures.

Example: When you are ready to talk about your family history, invite another family member over and at some point in the evening just start talking about good memories of growing up. As you all are sharing moments and are sharing laughs, share similar qualities or talents that are common in the family line and build from there. Talk to them about their grandparents and the kind of people they were. I would even suggest, especially if you aren't completely educated on your family's history, make it a family exploration and discover together. Be creative and intentional.

- Be attentive and walk through open doors.
  - o Life will always present moments that can be used to share a lesson. It is more important to know your child than it is to know what they are doing. Knowing your child will always let you know what they are doing. When you see small changes that are contrary to who they are, not who you want them to be, cleverly inquire.

Example: You have noticed that your child has been a lot of time on the phone with what sounds like the same person. They are happy and jolly and secretive at the same time. It appears to be that they have found a crush. All of a sudden they are not on the phone anymore and now they aren't as jovial. This is an opportunity to discuss relationships and emotions without ever mentioning what you have noticed. Take some time and take them on a date night. Over dinner or after a movie share with them some of your experiences using the date as a center-piece for the discussion.

- Set boundaries.
  - o Every child needs to be instructed and have parameters set in order to understand the dynamics of life. These conversations are the ones

that are intentional and concise.

Example: Your child is requesting
permission to participate in an activity (i.e.
football team, cheerleading, and
gymnastics). Discuss with the child the
responsibilities that accompany their
involvement in the activity. These
responsibilities should be those that are
both directly and indirectly connected to
the event. If the child has a uniform, it is
their responsibility to be sure that it is
cared for and in the proper place so that it
can be washed in enough time prior to the
next time it is to be worn. Create a
contract that lays out the responsibilities
and include yourself and your

responsibilities as well (i.e. assuring timely arrival and departure to and from events pertaining to the activity, etc.). Be sure to include consequences for both parent and child as well.

Parenting is an exciting process and its rewards are great but the greatest reward is seeing your child develop and grow to become the most beautiful extension of you. It is the most selfless role in life. It is your opportunity to impact the world. Never underestimate the power of your presence and the influence of your love. Do not take for granted the opportunity and the gift you have in being a parent. Remember balance. Don't become what you have once despised. Infect your child with knowledge and the tools they need to excel. Sit back and enjoy

the ride!

www.ingramcontent.com/pod-product-compliance
Lightning Source LLC
Chambersburg PA
CBHW072007040426

42447CB00009B/1521